NATIONAL GEOGRAPHIC

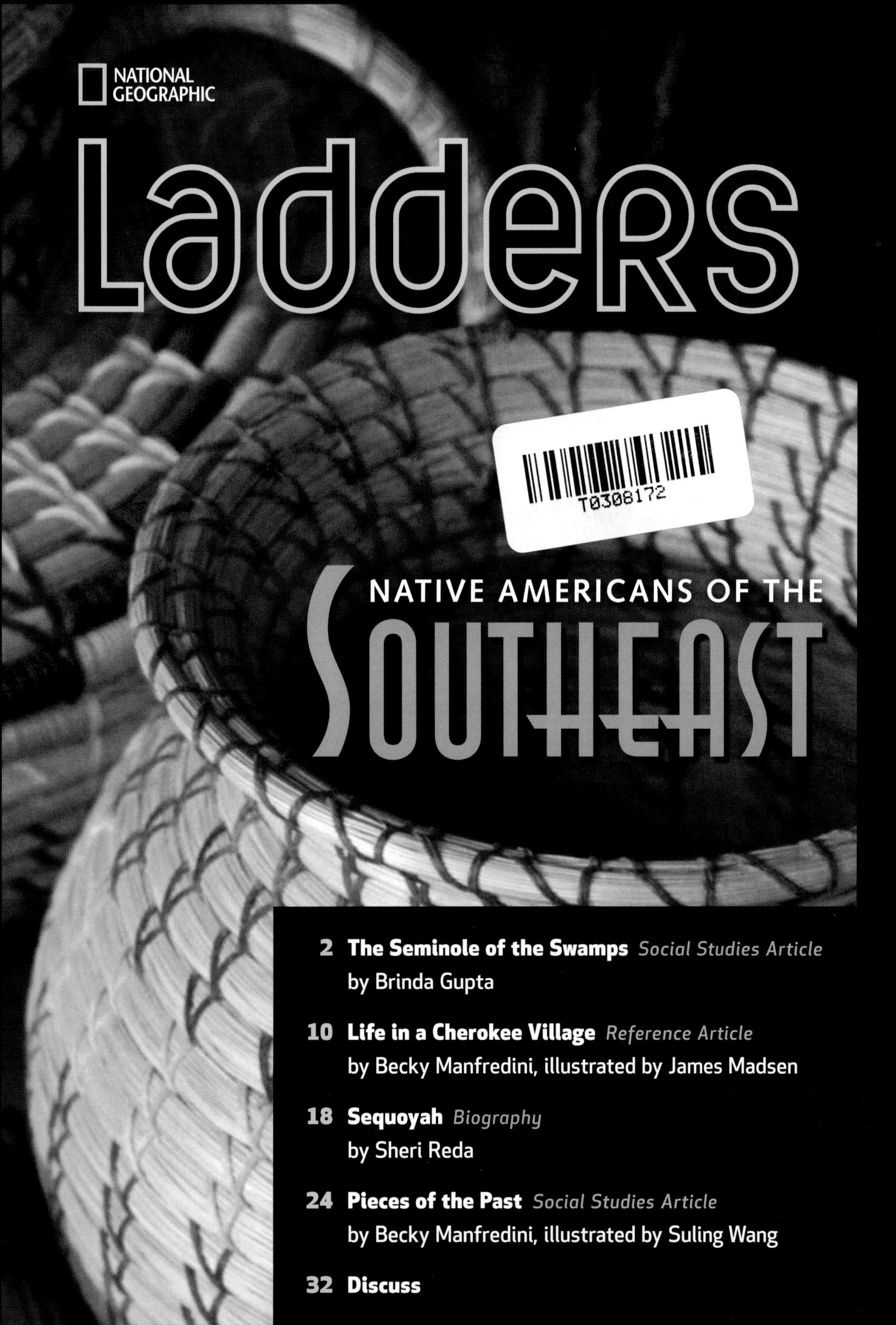

Ladders

Native Americans of the Southeast

GENRE **Social Studies Article**

Read to find out how the geography and climate of Florida affected the lives of the Seminole.

THE SEMINOLE OF THE SWAMPS

by Brinda Gupta

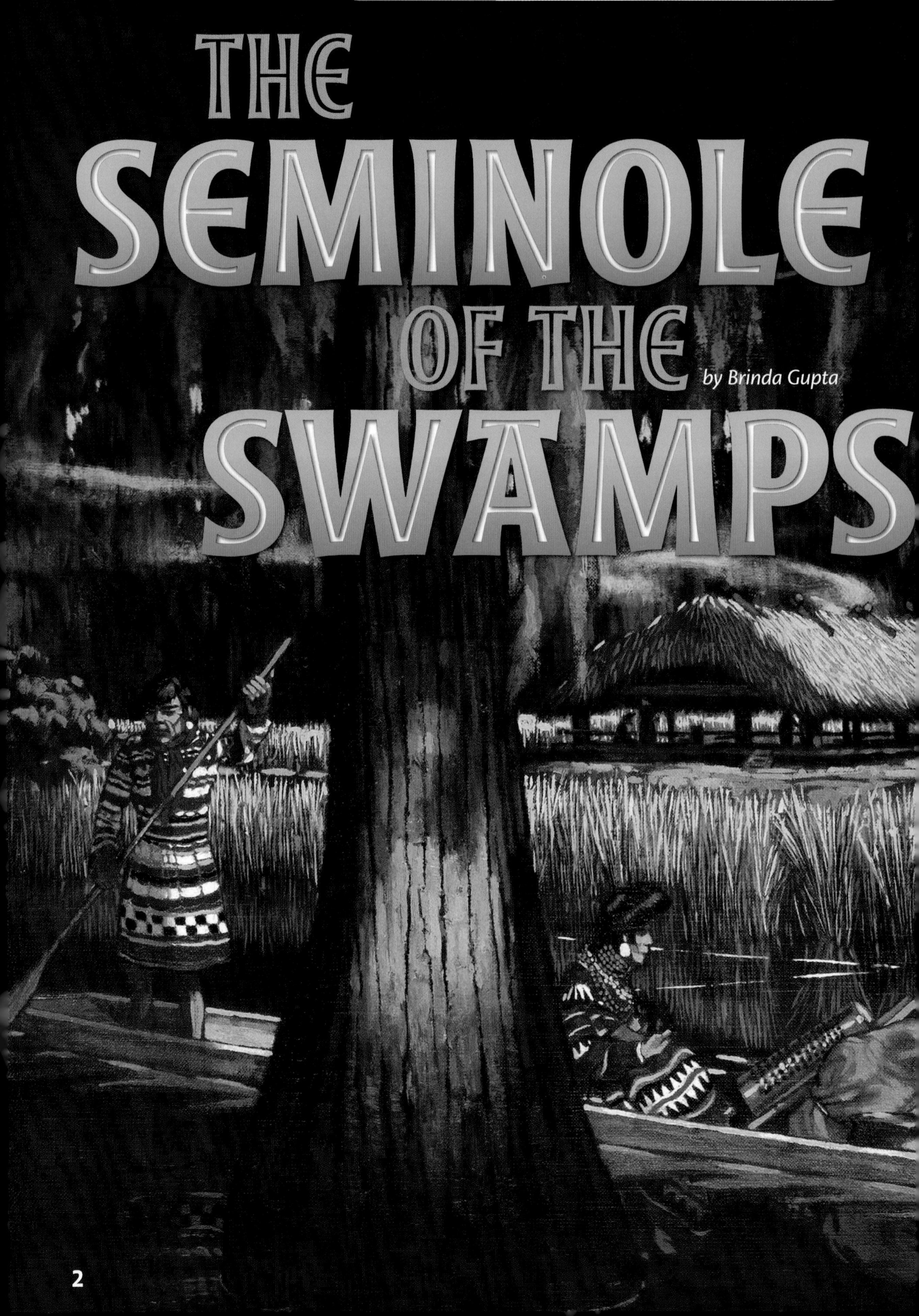

Northern and southern states have different **climates**. Climate, or average weather over time, affects the way you live. If you live in the northern United States, you know how to dress for cold weather. You probably have a lot of warm clothes. But if you live in the southern part of the country, you might just need a light jacket for winter. Climate affects how you live, and it affected how early Native Americans lived, too.

The Seminole are Native Americans who lived in Florida's warm climate in the 1700s. They are a mix of different Native American groups. The mix also includes African Americans who tried to escape slavery. These people all came together to form one tribe. The Seminole adapted their lives to the steamy swamps and tropical climate they lived in.

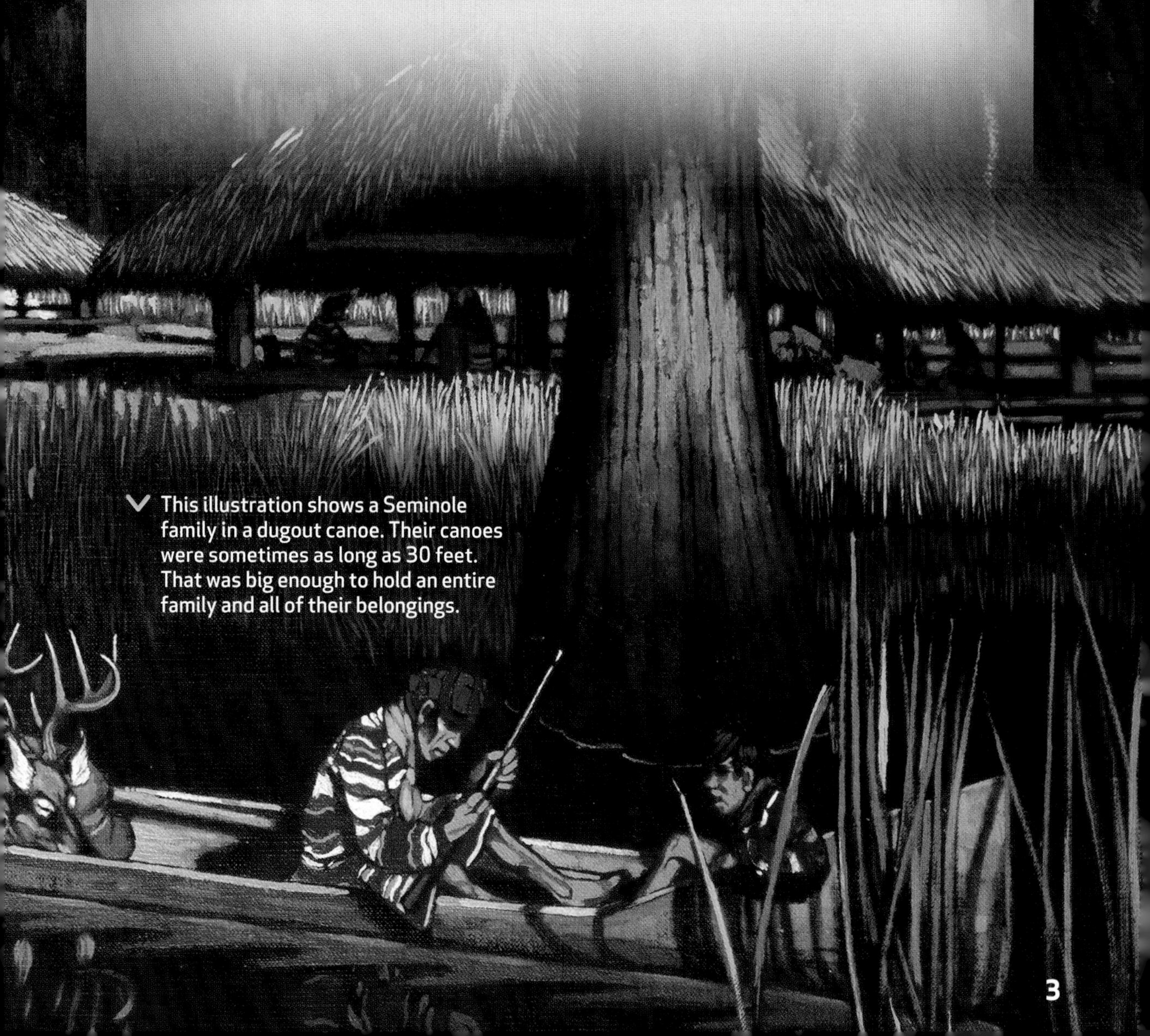

This illustration shows a Seminole family in a dugout canoe. Their canoes were sometimes as long as 30 feet. That was big enough to hold an entire family and all of their belongings.

BEATING THE HEAT

Florida has two climates. Northern Florida has a subtropical climate. It has hot, wet summers and mild winters. Southern Florida is hot all year. It has a tropical climate. It gets a lot of rain, including hurricanes. The Seminole and other tribes lived in southern Florida despite the extreme weather.

You might think that all Native Americans lived in tipis, or tent homes. Tipis were covered with buffalo hides to keep people warm inside. But the Seminole didn't need to keep warm. They needed homes that could keep them cool and dry.

Traditionally, the Seminole lived in huts called *chickees*. Chickees were open on the sides to let breezes blow through. Thatched roofs protected families from the hot sun and heavy rains. The Seminole built their chickees among **hammocks**, areas of land that rise over grassy swamps. Because the land could flood in heavy rain, chickees were raised on stilts to stay dry.

Long ago, the Seminole used local materials to make chickees like this reconstruction. They used wood from cypress trees to make poles that held up the roof. They wove palm fronds, or leaves, together to make the roof. Chickees were easy to build. They stayed cool and dry in the swampland.

TRAVELING THROUGH WETLANDS

The Seminole lived near swamps now called the Everglades. To move about the area, they could walk or canoe. When walking, the Seminole followed animal trails through the hammocks. For quicker travel, they moved through the waterways in canoes.

The Seminole used special canoes called dugout canoes, which they made from the logs of cypress trees. They used poles to push these canoes through water. Poles worked better than paddles because the swampy waterways were shallow. The poles allowed canoers to push off the bottom to move along, or if they got stuck.

The Everglades had many dangers. Poisonous snakes hid in the grasses, and alligators lurked below the water's surface. Though alligators can travel on land, they spend most of their time in swamps. The Seminole learned to respect these and other animals. They gave them space as they canoed through the Everglades.

The Seminole still build dugout canoes. However, the biggest cypress trees were cut down years ago. So modern Seminole canoes are smaller than the traditional canoes.

This modern Seminole uses a pole to push his dugout canoe. The ancestors of the Seminole made and used dugout canoes as far back as 5,000 years ago.

FISH AND FRUIT

The Seminole got much of their food from the water. Standing in their canoes, they speared fish. They also collected snails and oysters. A Seminole brave enough to hunt an alligator could make a meal from its cooked meat. In forests nearby, the Seminole hunted deer, rabbits, and turkeys.

The region's climate was perfect for picking wild berries and growing fruits such as pumpkins, pineapples, and oranges. The Seminole had vegetables such as beans and squash. They also grew corn and sugarcane. A Seminole meal may have included fish with rice and sweet potatoes, cornbread, and a salad of bananas and grapes. The Seminole had to live through some hot days, but they would never run out of food.

HEALTHY EATERS

The Seminole had a delicious and varied diet. Corn and flour made from ground corn were ingredients in many of their meals. Even some of their drinks contained corn. They also ate a lot of veggies, like the yellow squash and green beans shown in this photo.

This Seminole woman uses a traditional wooden tool to grind corn for cooking. The tool is called a mortar and pestle. The mortar is the container where the corn is ground. The pestle is the large pole she is using to grind the corn.

Check In How did the Seminole adapt to living in the tropical climate of southern Florida?

GENRE **Reference Article** **Read to find out** about life in a Cherokee village.

Life in a Cherokee VILLAGE

by Becky Manfredini illustrated by James Madsen

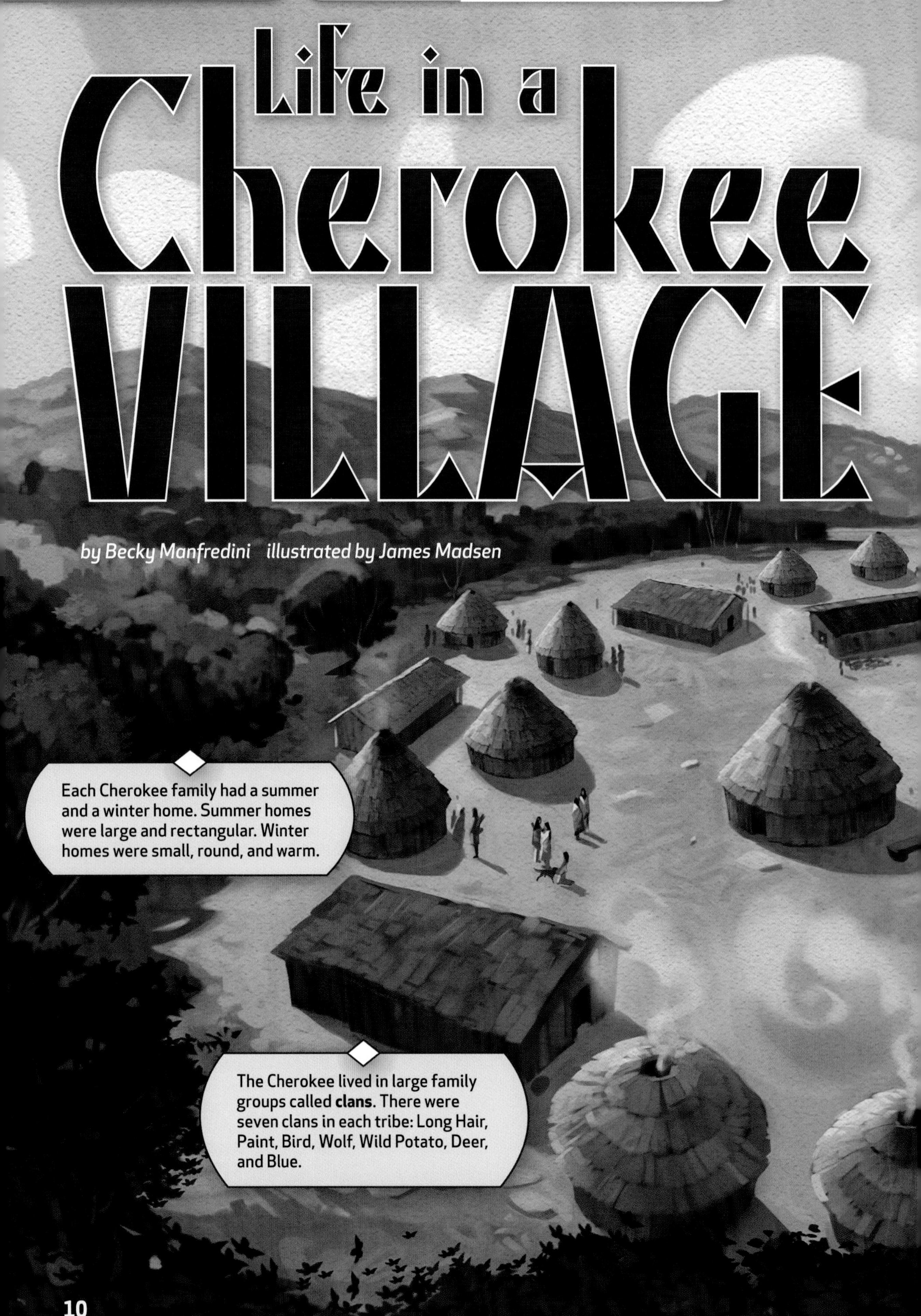

Each Cherokee family had a summer and a winter home. Summer homes were large and rectangular. Winter homes were small, round, and warm.

The Cherokee lived in large family groups called **clans**. There were seven clans in each tribe: Long Hair, Paint, Bird, Wolf, Wild Potato, Deer, and Blue.

Imagine living beside a river in the region we now know as the states of Georgia, Tennessee, North Carolina, and South Carolina. There are forests all around you. Your home is one of 40 in a village where more than 400 people live. You do your chores and then play games with other children. Your mother plants corn, and your father carves hunting tools.

That's what life was like for the Cherokee people. The Cherokee are a Native American people who lived in the foothills of the Appalachian Mountains in the southeastern United States. Foothills are the low parts of a mountain range. Some Cherokee still live in this region. But most Cherokee were forced to move west in the 1830s.

Each Cherokee village had a **plaza**, or public square, in its center. The plaza was used for meetings, trading, and religious ceremonies.

Home and Hearth

Cherokee villages were busy all year. The Cherokee farmed in summer and hunted in winter. Men cleared the fields to plant crops, but women grew the food. Boys wrestled, played games, and used small bows and arrows to shoot at squirrels and rabbits. Girls helped their mothers with chores. They learned to run a household.

CHEROKEE VILLAGE
Men built canoes and the village's buildings. They also helped with the harvest.
In winter, the men hunted deer, turkey, and bear. The Cherokee used every part of these animals. They ate the meat, made clothing from skins, and made tools from antlers and bones.

Cherokee men cut down trees with axes. The axes had blades made of stone and handles made of bone. The men built dugout canoes from the tree trunks. To make the canoes, they burned out the logs' centers and scraped away the charred wood.
The Cherokee caught fish with **weirs**, underwater traps made of stone and branches. They also fished with spears and nets.

By the Water

The Cherokee built their villages near water. They used the water for drinking, cooking, and bathing. The waterways also gave them a way to travel in canoes and trade goods. After Europeans moved onto their land, the Cherokee traded their deerskins for the Europeans' metal tools, guns, glass, and cloth.

Water wasn't just for hunting and drinking. Cherokee children loved to swim, splash around, and cool off in the water.

Cherokee women gathered reeds, or the tall grasses along the rivers, to make baskets. The baskets were used for storing and carrying food and firewood.

In the Plaza

Today, people go to malls, theaters, and grocery stores to buy things and to see friends. For the Cherokee, the plaza was *the* place to be. They came there to spend time together, hold meetings, dance, and celebrate.

On holidays, the Cherokee lit a fire in the plaza to celebrate. A person called the Firekeeper kept the fire burning.

The Council House was a large circular building in the plaza. They held meetings there. Villagers sat on benches in this building to hear the elder Cherokee women and men have discussions and make decisions. One important village decision might be whether or not to go to war.

At sundown during holidays, people danced the Stomp Dance in the plaza. This is a religious and social dance. It has been a part of Cherokee life for hundreds of years. People called shell shakers shake rattles on their legs made of pebbles and shells. They make a rhythm by shuffling their feet. The dancers circle the fire, dancing to the rhythm.

Check In What types of work did men and women do in a traditional Cherokee village?

GENRE Biography

Read to find out about Sequoyah's accomplishments.

Se

quoyah

by Sheri Reda

Sequoyah (sih-KWOY-yuh) was a Cherokee leader with two names. Sequoyah was his Cherokee name. George Guess was his English name. Because his father was a white trader and his mother was Cherokee, Sequoyah grew up in two cultures. Yet he was respected by all. Sequoyah was so highly honored that the tallest trees in the country were named after him.

Sequoyah was born in the Cherokee village of Taskigi in Tennessee sometime between 1760 and 1775. His mother raised him and his two brothers. He became a trader and a **silversmith**. A silversmith makes items such as knives out of silver and other metals.

Sequoyah fought in the U.S. Army during the Creek War of 1813–1814. The war was fought mainly between Native American tribes. But the United States also took part in it. This event changed Sequoyah's life. Keep reading to find out how.

Sequoyah sat for this portrait during a visit to Washington, D.C. He came to Washington, D.C., to sign a peace treaty between the Cherokee people and the U.S. government.

The Inventor

When he was in the army, Sequoyah saw American soldiers writing letters and recording events. He thought that the secret to the Americans' power was writing. At that time, the Cherokee had no written language. Their knowledge depended on memorization. Sequoyah shared his idea about creating a written Cherokee language with some friends. But they had doubts about his idea.

After leaving the army, Sequoyah got married and had a family. He remained interested in writing. Sequoyah knew that Native Americans passed their cultures down to younger generations by telling stories. He also knew that writing was an easier way to pass information to future generations.

Sequoyah first tried to create a written Cherokee language in 1809. He made a symbol for each Cherokee word, but there were too many symbols. Sequoyah asked his daughter Ayoka for help. Together, they identified 85 different sounds in the Cherokee language. Then Sequoyah created a symbol for each of the sounds. Finally, he combined the symbols into words.

Sequoyah's writing system is called a syllabary (SIH-luh-bur-ee) because each symbol stands for a syllable in the Cherokee language. In English, each symbol stands for a letter.

ᎠᎳᏑᎶ

SHOE

The Cherokee word for shoe is *alasulo* (ah-lah-SOO-lo), but moccasins like these are *tsulawa* (tsoo-LAH-wah).

ᏬᎱᎾᏫ

TURTLE

Do you think that this eastern box turtle knows that it's called a *daksi* (DAHK-see) in Cherokee?

ᏔᎷᏣ

BASKET

The Cherokee word for basket is *talutsi* (tah-LOO-tsee). This traditional basket is woven from honeysuckle vine.

ᎠᏣᏗ

FISH

One Cherokee word for fish is *atsadi* (aht-SAHD-ee). They also have words for different kinds of fish. A trout is an *uga* (OO-GAH).

The Legacy

In 1821, Sequoyah and his daughter defended their writing system before the Cherokee Tribal Council. The council thought the system might be "witchcraft." Council members placed Sequoyah and Ayoka in separate rooms. They had Sequoyah write messages and then brought them to Ayoka. She quickly read and answered Sequoyah's messages.

Council members saw that there was no magic. They approved the writing system. Within a week, the council learned to read and write Cherokee. Within months, much of the Cherokee nation could read and write in its own language.

ᏡᎬ

TREE

Sequoia trees grow to heights of 300 feet or more. That's about the height of the Statue of Liberty or a 30-story building.

In 1825, the Cherokee honored Sequoyah with a silver medal and a lifetime **salary**. Sequoyah next decided to publish a newspaper in Cherokee and English. In 1828, the *Cherokee Phoenix* became the first newspaper printed in a Native American language.

When Sequoyah died in 1843, people all over the world mourned his death. He gave the Cherokee the gifts of reading and writing. He gave the gift of Cherokee stories to the world.

> More than ten years after Sequoyah's death, a scientist honored him by naming the giant California redwood trees after him. Sequoyah's great deedstruly made him a "giant."

Check In Why was Sequoyah so important to the Cherokee?

GENRE **Social Studies Article**

Read to find out about the pottery of the Native Americans of the Southeast.

PIECES of the Past

by Becky Manfredini
illustrated by Suling Wang

You're hiking along a trail when you see bits of broken pottery. You pick up these **shards** and wonder where they came from. You also wonder who used them and how they were used. If you enjoy putting together a puzzle like this, you might like to learn about **archaeology** (ahr-kee-OL-uh-jee). Archaeologists study artifacts, or objects from the past, to learn how people lived long ago.

About 4,000 years ago, Native Americans of the Southeast began making pottery. Different Native American tribes had their own styles of pottery and decorations, which they painted on the pottery.

Archaeologists collected all the shards shown below. Then they pieced them together to reveal the original form of a pot.

If you saw these shards, how would you know they were pieces of broken pottery? Archaeologists look at the edges and the pattern on the shard to be sure it was from a pot and not just a rock.

From the Earth

Native Americans used pottery for many purposes. They used pottery containers for storing, cooking, and serving food and drinks. They gave pottery as gifts. They also used pottery for religious reasons.

Pottery is made of clay, a sticky kind of earth. Clay is soft when it's wet, and you can shape it. It hardens when it dries or when you bake it in an oven. Native American potters **tempered** the clay, or made it stronger, by mixing it with other materials. People on the coast used crushed shells or sand to temper their pots. Potters near the forest used crushed animal bones. People near streams and rivers used pebbles. Some potters used pieces of old pots to temper new pots.

Native Americans of the Southeast still make pottery today. Some tribes decorate their work with patterns. Other tribes carve or paint animals or people onto the pottery.

Native American potter Sweeny Willis made this pot using a coiling method.

Mississippian

Mississippian people lived near the Mississippi River. They painted and carved designs on clay jars, plates, and pots. They used shells to temper their pottery. They made some pots in the shape of a human head. They left these pots when they buried their dead. The pots are from about A.D. 700.

This Mississippian pitcher was crafted into the form of a woman with a tattooed face.

This Pamunkey bowl was made in the early 1900s. It represents a man wearing a feather headdress.

Pamunkey

The Pamunkey tribe of northeastern Virginia traded pottery to European settlers in the 1600s. Their pottery was made with dark river clay. They made bowls, pipes, and other containers.

Cherokee

Almost 2,000 years ago, the Cherokee of Tennessee and North Carolina began making "stamped pottery." Potters stamped their pottery using wooden paddles that had designs carved into them.

A modern-day Cherokee artist crafted this stamped pottery.

Catawba

For thousands of years, the Catawba of South and North Carolina have made pottery of dark clay. The wood in the baking fires causes the pottery to be streaked with beige, brown, or gray. Some Catawba potters make bowls in the shape of animals.

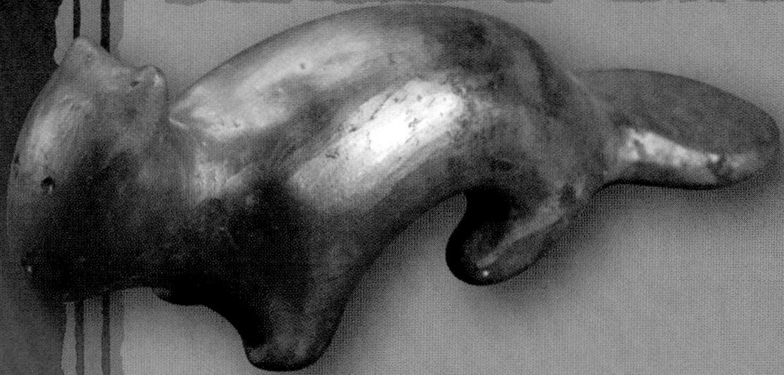

The modern Catawba artist who made this beaver polished it to make it shine.

This modern streaked Catawba vessel features a human face.

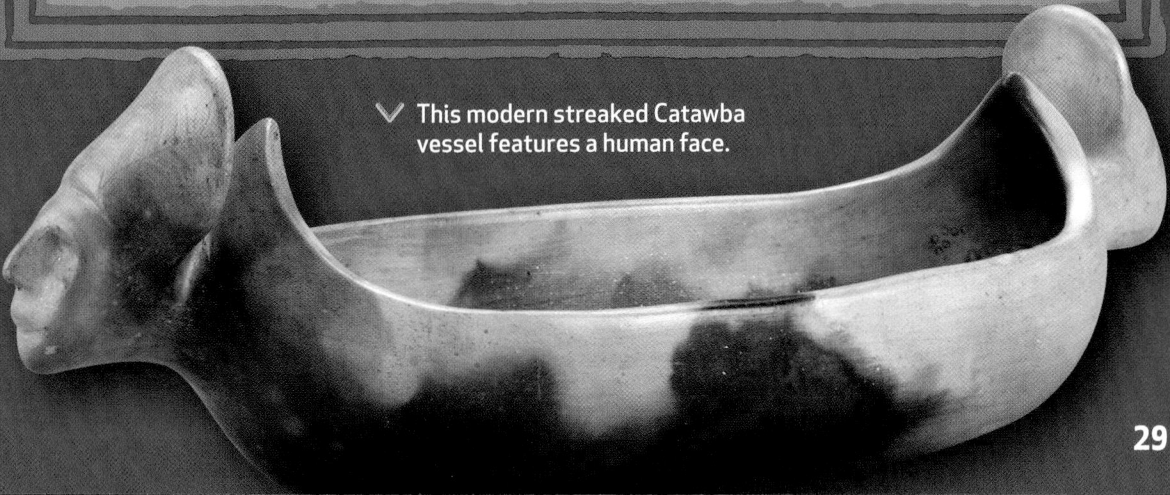

Making Pottery

If you lived long ago, here's how you might have made a pot.

1 **SOFTEN THE CLAY:** Prepare a lump of clay for shaping. Add water. Then **knead** it, or work it with your hands, until it's soft.

2 **TEMPER:** Add a handful of pebbles, sand, or crushed shells.

5 **SMOOTH:** Use your fingers to smooth the sides of the container, inside and out.

6 **DRY:** Place your clay object in the sun to dry it. Depending on how dry the air is, this step could take up to two weeks!

3 ROLL: Make smaller lumps of clay. Roll each one into a long coil.

4 FORM AND STACK: Form the coils into circles. Stack the circles on top of each other to form a container.

7 PAINT: Paint a design on it that tells something about your way of life.

8 BAKE: Put your object in a kiln, or pottery oven. When it's dry, you will have your own piece of pottery.

Check In What is the most interesting information you've learned about the pottery of the southeastern Native Americans?

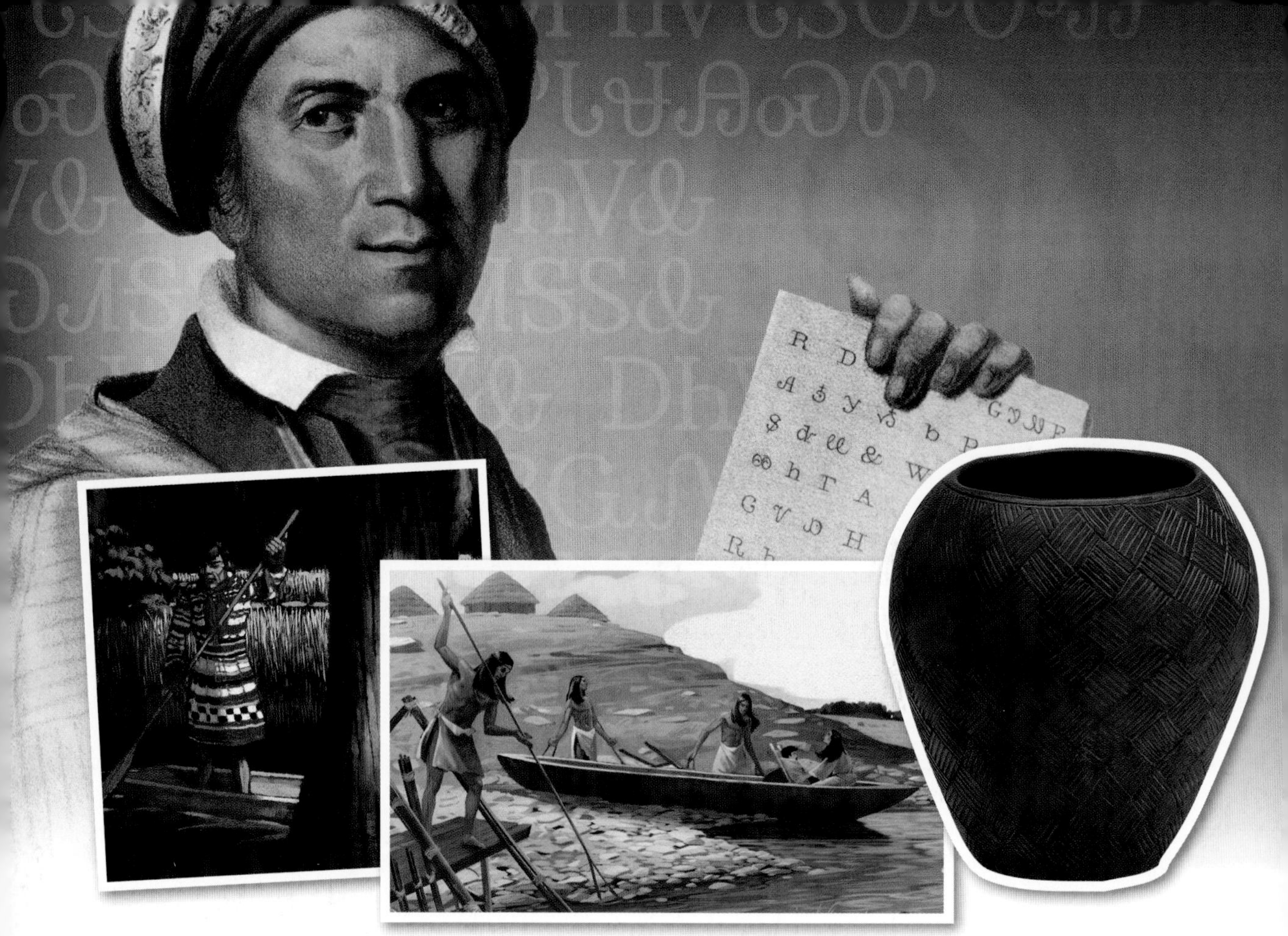

Discuss

1. What connections can you make among the four selections in this book? How do you think the selections are related?

2. How do you think the writing system that Sequoyah invented would benefit the Cherokee?

3. Describe the traditional Cherokee way of life, including their jobs, pastimes, and community events. How does the Cherokee way of life of long ago compare to your life today?

4. What can archaeologists learn about Native Americans of the Southeast by studying shards of broken pottery?

5. What would you still like to find out about the Native Americans of the Southeast?